PREHISTORIC LIFE

THE FIRST PEOPLE

RUPERT MATTHEWS

Artist: Jonathon Heap

Titles in this series

How Life Began

The Dinosaur Age

The Age of Mammals

Ice Age Animals

The First People

The First Settlements

Cover illustration: Neanderthal people making stone tools.

Editor: Alison Cooper
Designer: Ross George
Consultant: John Cooper B.Sc., A.M.A., F.G.S.

First published in 1990 by
Wayland (Publishers) Ltd
61 Western Road, Hove
East Sussex, BN3 1JD, England

British Library Cataloguing in Publication Data
Matthews, Rupert
    The first people.
    1. Prehistoric man
    I. Title. II. Series
    930.1

ISBN 1-85210-728-6

Typeset by Direct Image Photosetting Ltd,
Hove, East Sussex, England
Printed by G. Canale & C.S.p.A., Turin, Italy
Bound by Casterman S.A., Belgium

Contents

Words printed in **bold** are explained in the glossary.

What is a Human?

The human being is a unique creature. Unlike all other animals, humans are not totally dependent on their surroundings. If the weather is too cold, people may build houses or gather round fires to keep warm. Farmers plant **crops** and gather in the harvest for food. Humans do not need to rely on finding food growing wild in fields and woods.

Humans have some control over their **environment**; animals can only live within it. This is mainly due to the large brain that humans have and their ability to think. It is because humans can solve problems by thinking about them that they have been able to achieve so much. The human body, by comparison, is rather weak. It is, for instance, no match for a tiger or a bull.

The clearest sign of humans' ability to think is their use of **tools**. A simple example of using tools is when a person uses a sharp knife to cut through a piece of meat. This is much easier than trying to chew through the meat with bare teeth. Other tools are far more complex. For example, machines such as motor cars enable people to travel further and faster than they can walk or run.

When studying the ancestors of modern humans, scientists are faced with several problems.

Below Was Homo habilis an ape or an early human?

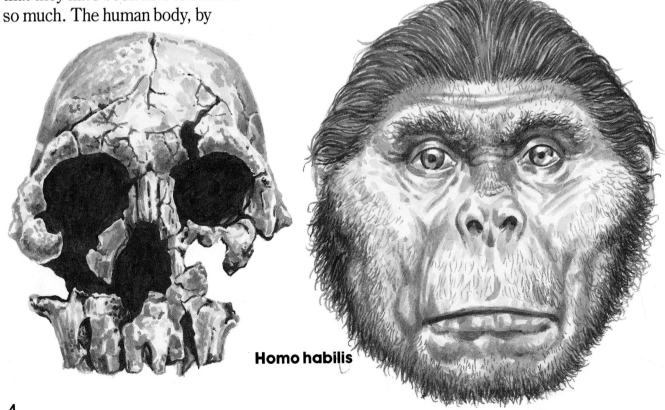

Homo habilis

Right **The fossilized jaw of Homo habilis. Scientists use fossils like this to create models of our ancestors.**

First, only a few **fossils** of human ancestors have been found. This means that scientists have little evidence on which to base their ideas about human **evolution**.

Another problem is that scientists need to decide if a fossil belongs to a primitive human or to a highly developed type of ape. Some scientists think that they can decide by measuring brain size. A modern human, for instance, has a brain of about 1,500 cc (cubic centimetres), while a chimpanzee has a brain of around 400 cc. If a man-like ape has a large brain, then it could be classed as a human. However, other scientists disagree.

They argue that an ancient ape should be classed as a human only if it used tools.

These differences of opinion can lead to confusion. For instance, a fossil found in Africa a few years ago is considered by some scientists to be human, so they call it Homo habilis, meaning 'handy man'. Other scientists think that it is an ape and have named it Australopithecus habilis, which means 'handy southern ape'. Such problems are common and only the discovery of more fossils may solve these disagreements. Scientists continue to search for fossils of ancient humans.

5

The First Primates

Modern humans are described scientifically as Homo sapiens sapiens, which means 'wise wise man'. They are grouped within the ape family along with gorillas and chimpanzees. Apes are part of the much larger group known as primates, which also includes monkeys and **lemurs**.

The very earliest primates lived about 70 million years ago, when **dinosaurs** such as Triceratops and Tyrannosaurus still lived on earth. These early primates looked rather like modern shrews. They lived in trees and probably ate fruit and insects.

One of the best known of these primates was Plesiadapis, which lived in North America about 60 million years ago. Plesiadapis had a long tail and looked rather like a squirrel. It was about 70 cm long and lived in forests. Although it was a primate, this creature did not have the grasping hand which developed in its **descendants**. It probably ran along the tops of branches, holding on with its sharp claws. Eventually, primates developed the ability to grip branches and to hang underneath them.

Plesiadapis

Right **Plesiadapis was one of the first primates. Like many of its descendants, it lived in trees.**

Later the primates divided into three main groups. The prosimians remained small and primitive. Modern prosimians include lemurs and **loris**. The second primate group, the apes, first evolved some 40 million years ago. They include the modern gibbon and gorilla. Humans evolved from a branch of the early apes. The third division of the primates includes all the monkeys. The monkeys evolved after the other primates but they spread rapidly across the world. They are divided into two main groups: the New World monkeys of the Americas and the Old World monkeys.

Left **The vervet belongs to the monkey family and lives in East Africa.**

Survivors of the primate past

The island of Madagascar separated from Africa before either apes or monkeys evolved. The prosimians have survived and developed on Madagascar, although they died out elsewhere. The most famous prosimians on the island are the lemurs. There are a number of different species. The ring-tailed lemur (right) is fairly small, but it has a long tail with black and white rings. The Indri is the largest lemur alive today, but until recently a species of lemur the size of a small pony lived on Madagascar.

7

Hominids

The ape family is divided into three smaller families. The great apes, including gorillas and chimpanzees, are known as the Pongids. The gibbons are grouped together in the family Hylobatidae. Humans belong to the Hominid family, and they are the only surviving members of that family. Scientists have been able to trace back some of these families for many millions of years.

The ape which scientists call Aegyptopithecus lived in North Africa about 30 million years ago. It was nearly 1m long and had many typical ape features. It had strong, grasping hands, which it used to grip tree branches. The eyes faced forwards, allowing the ape to judge distances more accurately. This ability was very important for an animal which spent much of its time jumping from branch to branch.

Below Some scientists believe that Ramapithecus is the earliest type of hominid ape.

One of the most interesting **theories** to account for the early evolution of the Hominids concerns the possible feeding habits of Ramapithecus. It is thought that this ape may have fed on small, hard objects, such as seeds and roots. To do this effectively, the creature would have sat upright and taken food to its mouth with its hands. This may have led to the evolution of animals that stood upright most of the time, instead of on all fours. At the same time, the need to grind up tough food would have created the broad, flat teeth of the Hominid apes.

Ramapithecus

After Aegyptopithecus died out, many different forms of ape evolved. However, it was not until about 14 million years ago that an ape appeared which may have belonged to the Hominid family. This creature is known as Ramapithecus, and there were several different species living in places as far apart as India, eastern Africa and Russia.

Ramapithecus was very similar to earlier apes, but it had some very hominid-like features. Its back teeth, for example, were wider and flatter than those of other apes, and it had short canine teeth. These are features which were shared by all later Hominid apes and by humans. Ramapithecus may also have been able to stand upright on its hind legs like modern apes, but it probably spent most of its time on all fours.

African Origins

Fossils of Hominids that lived immediately after Ramapithecus are very rare. Scientists have been unable to find fossils dating from between 10 million and 5 million years ago. We do not know what evolutionary changes occurred during this time.

However, we do know that about 5 million years ago a creature lived in Africa which scientists have named Australopithecus africanus, which means 'southern ape of Africa'. This creature was very much more like a human than earlier Hominid apes had been. It stood about 1.3 m tall and walked upright, though perhaps not as efficiently as modern humans. Australopithecus had a flat face, instead of the projecting snout of earlier apes. It had a brain size of 450 cc, rather larger than a modern chimpanzee. Although it was very human in appearance, there is no evidence that Australopithecus could use tools, so it cannot be classified as human.

By about 2.5 million years ago, a new type of Australopithecus had appeared alongside the africanus species. This has been given the name robustus. This creature was much larger and heavier than africanus. It stood over 1.7 m tall and may have weighed twice as much as the africanus.

Some robustus skulls have a crest of bone running along the top of the skull. Strong jaw muscles were attached to this ridge. This seems to indicate that robustus may have eaten tougher food than africanus did. Some scientists have suggested that robustus ate tough plant food, which would have required strong jaw muscles, while africanus ate at least some meat.

The robustus and africanus forms lived side by side in Africa for over a million years. The later forms of robustus were even larger and heavier than before.

Below About 2 million years ago two different types of Hominid ape lived in Africa.

Australopithecus robustus

Some scientists think that such creatures were so different from Australopithecus africanus that they should be given a new name. They call this form Paranthropus robustus. The robustus form survived until about 1.5 million years ago. Then it died out. Scientists do not think it left any descendants.

The africanus type survived for much longer than the robustus. Eventually it evolved into new forms of Hominid. It is even possible that the very first humans evolved from it.

Left **Scientists working on excavations at Sterkfontein, South Africa, where several Hominid fossils have been found.**

Australopithecus africanus

The First Humans

For scientists, the period of time between the appearance of Australopithecus africanus and the first examples of Homo erectus is rather confusing. Experts are not certain how the fossils that have been found fit into the process of human evolution.

Some fossils consist of only a few pieces of skull. Others are more complete but seem to contradict the evidence of other finds. One of these fossils was found by Dr Louis Leakey in Tanzania, and dates back nearly 2 million years. The fossils revealed a creature which was rather similar to Australopithecus africanus, but which had a brain size of 650 cc. Alongside the fossil bones were several simple stone tools. The hands of the creature would clearly have been able to grip and use such tools. Dr Leakey believed he had found a primitive Hominid which used tools. He gave the name Homo habilis, meaning 'handy man' to his find. He claimed that this was the oldest known human.

In 1972 an even older fossil skull was found in Kenya. This skull was larger than that of Homo habilis and was also found together with tools. Some scientists think that this new skull represents the earliest human, but others believe that Homo habilis is the earliest. Some scientists think that neither of these creatures can really be described as human. They think that the fossils represent only a highly-developed form of Australopithecus. Further fossil finds might help scientists to understand more clearly how humans evolved.

Right **An Homo habilis using a primitive stone tool.**

The Piltdown hoax

In 1912 a skull was found at Piltdown in Sussex, England. This skull was thought to show a creature with a human-sized brain, but an ape-like jaw. Scientists now know that the skull is a fake, but for many years people believed that it was genuine. Scientists thought that the Piltdown skull proved that humans first evolved as intelligent apes.

When other fossils, such as Australopithecus, revealed human-like creatures with small skulls, scientists refused to believe that they were genuine early Hominids. Only when the Piltdown **hoax** was revealed in 1953 did people realize how important these other fossils really were to the study of human evolution.

Homo habilis

Above **The famous scientist Dr Mary Leakey working at the Olduvai Gorge site in Tanzania. The Leakey family have discovered many important fossils.**

Upright Humans

The earliest fossils that are generally accepted as belonging to a human are those known as Homo erectus, which means 'upright man'. Fossils of Homo erectus have been found across Asia, Europe and Africa. Clearly the species was very successful and numerous.

The first Homo erectus fossils to be discovered came from **Java**. Many people still call this human species 'Java man'. The fossils were found by a Dutch professor named Eugène Dubois. In 1891 Java was governed by the Dutch, so Dubois

easily gained permission to work on the island. In 1891-2, Dubois found several fossilized bones dating back about 500,000 years.

We now know that Homo erectus first appeared about a million years ago. It stood about 1.6 m tall and had a very human-like body. The leg bones of Homo erectus show that it walked and ran in precisely the same way as modern humans. In fact, most of the differences between Homo erectus and ourselves are to be found in the creature's skull.

Below A map showing the places where scientists have found fossils of Homo erectus. This type of human never reached Australia or America.

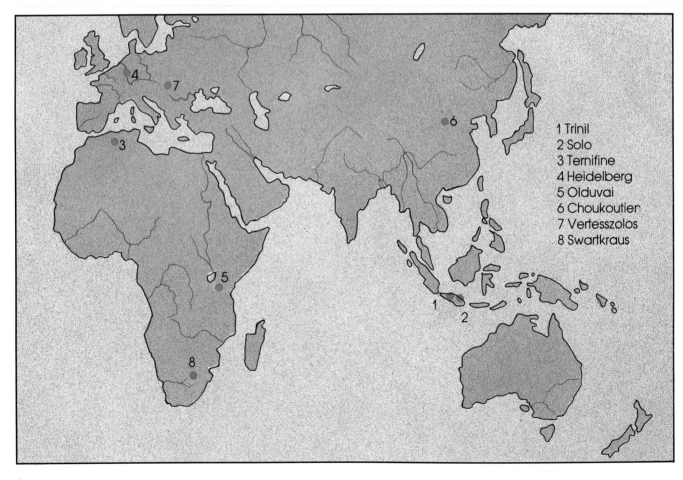

1 Trinil
2 Solo
3 Ternifine
4 Heidelberg
5 Olduvai
6 Choukoutien
7 Vertesszolos
8 Swartkraus

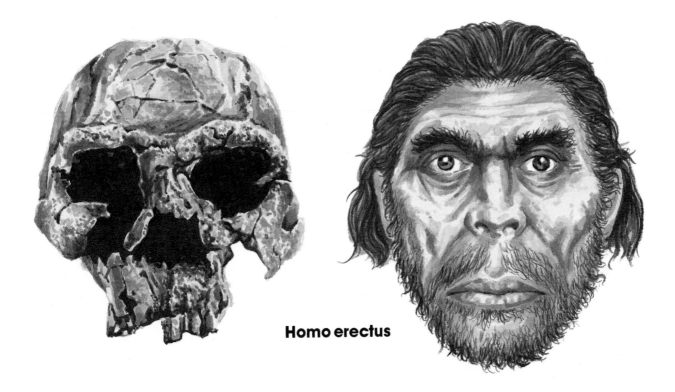

Homo erectus

The face of Homo erectus was very different from that of modern man. The forehead sloped back so sharply that it was almost non-existent. Over the eyes there was a very thick band of bone, creating a heavy **brow-ridge**. The lower jaw was heavy and broad, but there was no proper chin. This meant that the mouth projected forwards. It looked similar to an animal's snout.

The skull bones of Homo erectus were thick and strong. The top of the skull was rather flat, though in more recent examples it is more dome-shaped. The brain capacity of these humans was only about 850 cc, just over half that of modern people. It seems that the earlier Homo erectus had a smaller brain and more pronounced brow-ridge than later types.

The upper jaws of some Homo erectus show a curious gap between the canines and the front teeth. The canine tooth of the lower jaw fits into this gap when the mouth is closed. Scientists are not certain why some Homo erectus should have such a feature while others do not. The teeth of this human were stronger and larger than those of modern humans. It seems that Homo erectus was able to eat very tough food.

Above A skull of an Homo erectus. The brain inside the skull was just over half the size of a modern human brain.

15

Fires and Tools

One of the most important links between Homo erectus and modern humans is the use of tools. Homo erectus was able to make sharp stone tools from pebbles. These could be used to cut plants or meat. They might even have been used as weapons when hunting animals for food.

The Homo erectus species formed into groups called **cultures**. Scientists are able to recognize these different groups by looking at the stone tools they produced. All tools of a similar age, made in a similar way, are said to belong to a particular culture. The earliest stone tools were very simple. They were made by knocking chips off a pebble until a sharp edge was produced. These tools belonged to the Abbevillian culture, which was first discovered at Abbeville in France.

In later cultures better tools were made. One of these cultures is called the Acheulian culture. Many Acheulian hand axes have been discovered. The hand axe consisted of a large, pear-shaped stone which was carefully worked to give a good cutting edge and to be comfortable in the hand. The flakes struck off when making a hand axe were also used as tools, perhaps as knives and scraping instruments.

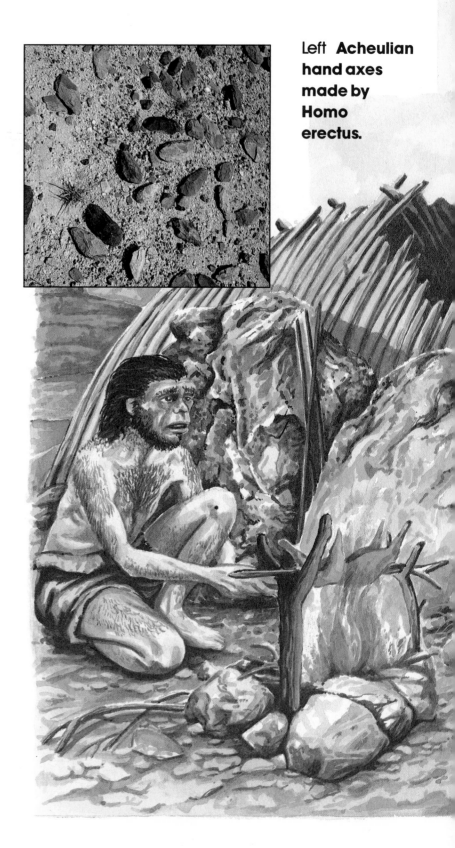

Left **Acheulian hand axes made by Homo erectus.**

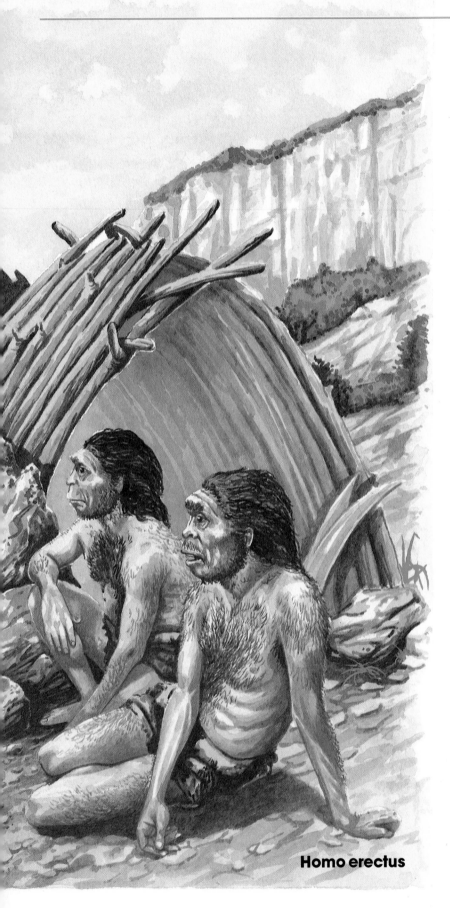

Homo erectus

Homo erectus also knew how to make fire. Several sites where Homo erectus lived contain **hearths** where fires were kept burning. One site in China revealed a fireplace with ashes piled to a depth of 6 m. The fire must have been kept burning for years to produce so much ash. Fires not only provided warmth in cold weather, but were probably used to cook food too. It is possible that pieces of meat were placed on sticks and held over the flames to roast. Homo erectus must have spent many evenings sitting round such blazes.

Later, groups of Homo erectus also built homes for themselves. Near Nice, in southern France, the remains of a wooden hut dating back to the time of Homo erectus have been found. The hut was made of **saplings** and tree branches which were bent to meet each other and form a roof. Large stones were placed around the outside of the hut for added strength. Scientists think that this particular hut was only used during the spring. Perhaps a family came to Nice each year because they knew that they could find certain foods there.

Left **A hut built by a band of Homo erectus in France.**

The Neanderthals

The first type of human, Homo erectus, survived for over 800,000 years. During that time, several different forms of Homo erectus developed. In general, the later forms had larger brains.

About 200,000 years ago, an entirely new type of human appeared. These people belonged to the same species as modern humans, Homo sapiens, but they still had some primitive features. The oldest fossils of these people were found at Steinheim in West Germany and at Swanscombe in Britain. The skulls of early Homo sapiens were more dome-shaped than those of earlier humans. The brow-ridges were smaller and the chin slightly more **prominent**. The brain case had a capacity of about 1,300 cc. This is almost the same as the average modern human brain.

Below The Neanderthals lived during the ice ages, when the weather was extremely cold.

By about 150,000 years ago these humans had evolved into the form which is known as Neanderthal man (Homo sapiens neanderthalensis). This type of early human was named after the German valley where the first fossils were recognized.

Neanderthal people were only slightly different from modern humans. They were rather short, standing about 1.7 m tall, but were very powerfully built. Neanderthal skeletons show that these people had strong muscles and very thick bones. The skull was rather long, with a lump at the back known as the occipital bun. The brain case had a capacity very similar to that of a modern human. Some Neanderthals had larger brains than modern humans! The face of a Neanderthal was very flat and had a wide nose.

Homo sapiens neanderthalensis

The First People

An Ice-Age Life Style

Homo sapiens neanderthalensis

The Neanderthal people lived during the later ice ages. This was a very difficult time for humans. It was very cold, of course. During the summer there would have been plenty of food in the form of nuts, fruit and leaves, but there was no food like this during the long, cold winters. The Neanderthals needed to be adaptable and cunning to cope with such conditions.

Neanderthal people probably lived in groups of about twenty individuals. The evidence we have about the way they lived shows that they co-operated with each other.

During the winter months, for instance, the men may have joined together to hunt large animals. Pits might have been dug as traps for deer or rhinoceros. Once an animal was caught, the men would have killed it with spears and sharp stones. Children might have been encouraged to catch smaller animals, such as hares or birds. By working together in this way, and constantly moving around in search of food, the Neanderthals would have been able to find enough to eat during the long, cold winters.

Neanderthals had several ways of keeping themselves warm. They certainly knew how to build fires. Small fireplaces have been found at most Neanderthal sites. These fires were kept blazing with wood

from the forests. The animals killed by Neanderthal hunters had furs which could be cut up and used as cloaks and clothes.

Neanderthal people also seem to have taken part in simple ceremonies. When one of their group died, they might have been buried in a grave and covered with flowers. This is another sign that members of the group co-operated with one another and that they cared for each other.

Above **Old men would teach the younger men how to split stones and make wooden spears.**

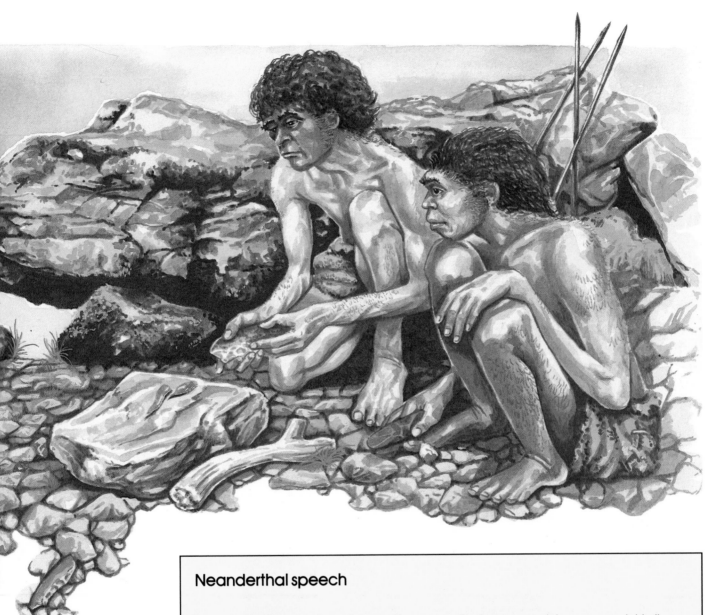

Neanderthal speech

In order to live and work together, Neanderthal people needed to pass information to each other. It seems that they were able to talk. The parts of their brains which controlled speech, and the voice boxes in their throats which help to make sounds, were better developed than in earlier humans.

Perhaps an old man would tell a young child how to make good stone tools. Hunters would have told each other about the movements of the prey animal. This would have made hunting much more efficient and ensured a better supply of food for the whole community.

The Flake Tools

Neanderthal people were skilled tool makers. One special technique that they invented is known as the Levalloisian technique. A stone, such as flint or crystal which splits easily, would be selected. First of all a large stone was selected. This was then carefully chipped and shaped until it became a domed oval. Several different tools could be made from this. By tapping the stone near its edges, long splinters could be struck off. These had very sharp sides and were a regular shape. Because it was prepared so carefully, several splinters could be taken from a single stone.

The people who belonged to the Mousterian culture produced a wide range of tools. Stone axes were still made, but they were of a better quality than those made by Homo erectus. Thin flakes with one sharp edge could be used as knives. Tools with tougher edges were made into scrapers.

Below The Neanderthals produced different tools for different tasks.

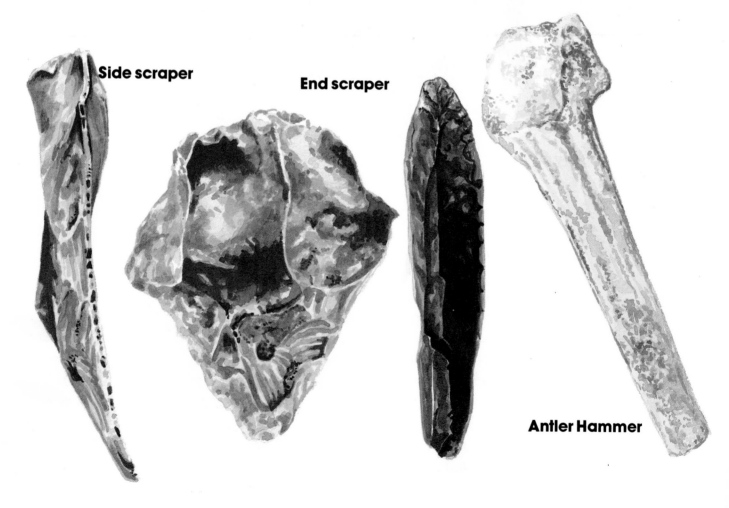

Side scraper

End scraper

Antler Hammer

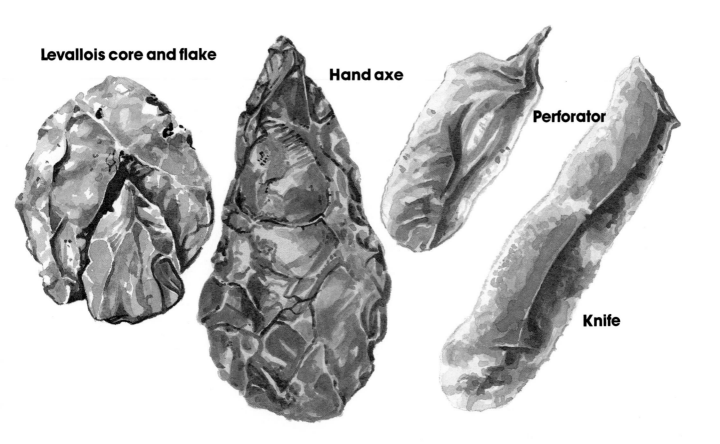

Levallois core and flake

Hand axe

Perforator

Knife

The scrapers might have been used to clean animal skins. The skins could then be made into clothes. Some tools were carefully shaped to give a sharp point. Perhaps they were used to drill holes in skins.

Most tools, such as hand axes and knives, were clearly intended to be used with the bare hands. However, some may have been fitted to a wooden handle. Some of the smaller tools might have been fitted to a long wooden pole to form a spear. Such a weapon would have made the Neanderthal a far more effective hunter. If such wooden handles ever existed, they have long since rotted away, leaving no traces behind.

There is also some evidence that Neanderthals used a form of bolas: this weapon is made of two stone weights tied together with a thin piece of leather. When thrown, it becomes entangled around the legs of a running animal. The creature trips and is unable to escape from the hunter.

Modern Humans

The Neanderthals belonged to the same species as modern humans, but still had primitive features such as a brow-ridge and a receding chin. Scientists are keen to discover the origin of the type of human that exists today, Homo sapiens sapiens.

Perhaps the best indication of where modern humans first evolved comes from caves on Mount Carmel in Israel. Bones found there are about 100,000 years old and are very different from the Neanderthal skeletons found in Europe. They are more like us than any previous form of human.

The people of Mount Carmel were about 1.7 m tall. The skulls found at the site were more dome-shaped than those of Neanderthals. They did not have the prominent brow-ridge and receding chin. The brain capacity of these people was the same as that of modern humans. The main difference between these people and ourselves is that they had slightly heavier skeletons.

It seems clear that modern humans are descended from the Mount Carmel people, who have been named Homo sapiens palestinus. This idea causes some problems. The Mount Carmel skeletons are as old as many Neanderthal finds in Europe.

The two types of human were living at the same time, but in different places. This seems to indicate that some time around 40,000 years ago, the descendants of the Mount Carmel people took over from the Neanderthals. We do not know if the Mount Carmel people's descendants invaded Neanderthal areas, so that the Neanderthal people were wiped out, or whether the two groups merged and bred with each other.

Finds from elsewhere in the world from this time are scarce.

Scientists are not certain whether Neanderthals lived in Africa, nor precisely when modern humans arrived on the continent. The humans of Southeast Asia seem to have belonged to a quite different type altogether. It is possible that these people evolved from Homo erectus independently of the people in Europe. Perhaps, in the future, finds of fossilized human remains will help scientists to discover exactly how modern humans evolved and how they spread across the world.

Below The earliest-known groups of modern humans lived in the Middle East.

Homo sapiens palestinus

The Mammoth Hunters

By about 40,000 years ago, a type of human almost the same as ourselves had appeared. These people lived throughout Asia, Europe and Africa. Later they spread to Australia, the Pacific islands and America. They developed different ways of life to cope with local conditions. One of the best known and exciting of these cultures was that of the mammoth hunters of Europe and Asia.

During the later part of the ice ages, vast herds of reindeer and elephant-like **mammoths** roamed through the forests and across the plains of Europe and Asia. These animals were hunted by people who belonged to the mammoth-hunter culture. Over the years the people killed large numbers of animals. At one camp the remains of more than a thousand mammoths have been found.

Below The mammoth hunters lived in central Europe.

The Plains Indians

Until the late nineteenth century a culture rather similar to that of the mammoth hunters existed on the plains of North America. Indian tribes – such as the Sioux, Blackfoot and Cheyenne – lived by hunting the enormous herds of buffalo which roamed the area. Everything needed by the Indians, from tents to clothing, was made from the bodies of the prey. Like the mammoth hunters, the Indians did not use metal. They used stone tools fitted on to wooden handles.

The creatures provided almost everything that was needed by the little community. The skins were made into clothes for protection against the cold. The bones could be made into tools and weapons. Leather could be made into thongs for sewing clothing or for use as string. Even the people's homes were made from the animals. Tusks, shoulder blades and leg bones were lashed together to form a framework. Over this were stretched skins and furs to form a tent-like structure. These houses could be several metres wide and were snug and warm.

The hunters were able to catch so many large animals because their culture was quite highly developed. They were skilled in the production of stone and bone tools. Many different types of tool were made for a variety of jobs. Some of these tools were fitted to wooden handles and may have been used as spears and axes.

It seems that several families lived together in a group. Perhaps a type of tribal society had developed by this time. These people co-operated in the hunting of large animals. Several men might have attacked a mammoth at once. Perhaps pits were dug to trap mammoths, or the creatures might have been driven into swamps.

Cave Art

Among the most surprising achievements of late prehistoric people were the artistic works which they produced. In many areas pieces of artwork which are thousands of years old have been discovered. They have a liveliness and beauty which amazed early researchers. At first, many scientists did not believe that prehistoric people could have been such fine artists. They thought the artwork dated from Roman or medieval times.

Possibly the most famous examples of such art are the cave paintings of France and Spain. Many painted caves, such as those at Lascaux and Altamira, have been discovered and studied. Most of the paintings are of animals which the people hunted for food. The pictures were painted with natural dyes in colours such as brown, red and black.

The paintings are very lifelike but most are tucked away deep in caves. No natural light can reach these dark corners. Some scientists think that this indicates that the paintings were not just for decoration, in the way that we hang pictures on walls today. Perhaps the paintings formed part of some ritual or magic. A few include arrows and spears. Perhaps the hunters thought that by painting a

picture of an animal, they would be more likely to catch the creature. It is possible that strange dances and ceremonies took place by firelight deep within the caves.

Paintings are not the only items that have been found. Scientists have also discovered many examples of engraving and carving. Several stones and bones were carved with pictures of animals. Some tools, such as spears, were decorated with pictures of animals. The hunters even made and wore jewellery. Beautiful necklaces and bracelets of shell and bone have been found in some burial places. The artistic work of prehistoric people took many different forms, and some very beautiful objects were produced.

Above **The prehistoric people of Australia painted this cave picture**

Right **Many caves in Europe contain beautiful paintings created by prehistoric people. Nobody is certain why the paintings were done.**

28

Homo sapiens sapiens

A stone age orchestra?

Recent excavations in eastern Europe have produced some very unusual finds. Decorated bones and antlers have been discovered that were worn in a very peculiar way. Some scientists have suggested that they were really musical instruments. The bones and antlers could have been knocked together to make drum-like noises. Objects which may have been whistles have also been found.

Glossary

Brow-ridge   A band of bone which projected forwards over the eyes in some types of prehistoric human.

Crop   A plant sown by humans in order to produce food. Wheat, carrots and potatoes are all crops.

Culture   A way of life shared by a group of people. Each group's way of life is slightly different to another group's. Scientists can divide the earliest humans into these culture groups only by looking at the different tools they used.

Descendant   A person or animal who is the child, grandchild or other direct relative of another person or animal. You are a descendant of your mother.

Dinosaurs   A group of large reptiles which dominated life on earth between 65 and 200 million years ago.

Environment   The various elements that make up a person's surroundings. In a town the environment consists of roads and buildings, in the country it consists of trees, fields and plants. The Arctic is a cold environment. A desert is a hot environment.

Evolution   The process by which all living things change and develop over a long period of time.

Fossil   The remains of a living object which have been turned into stone and preserved in rock.

Hearth   The place where a fire is made.

Hoax   A deception or trick.

Java   A large island between Australia and Malaysia.

Lemur   A type of small, tree-living primate found in Madagascar.

Loris   Slow-moving primates which sleep during the day and are active at night.

Mammoth   An extinct form of elephant.

Prominent   Standing out. Your nose is a prominent feature of your face.

Sapling   A young tree.

Theory   An idea put forward to try to explain certain facts.

Tool   An object used to make a task easier.

Books to read

Chierlova, Margot (trans) **Prehistoric Man, the dawn of our species** (Hamlyn, 1980)
Penny, Malcolm **Animal Evolution** (Wayland, 1987)
Sklenar, Karel **Hunters of the Stone Age** (Hamlyn, 1988)

Watson, Lucille **An Ice Age Hunter** (Wayland, 1986)
Anthology **The Rise of Man** (Grisewood and Dempsey, 1986)

Picture acknowledgements

The photographs in this book were supplied by: Bruce Coleman Ltd by the following photographers: R. I. M. Campbell 13, David Hughes 11, Kim Taylor 16; Geoscience Features Picture Library by W. Hughes 29; Oxford Scientific Films by the following photographers: Mark Pidgeon 7 (bottom), Frank Schneidermeyer 5, 7 (top).

Index